Tear ⟨  ⟩e

Adaı ⸱ɹrickson

graft
poetry

2011

Published 2011
Reprint 2013
Graft Poetry
Frizingley Hall
Frizinghall Road
Bradford
BD9 4LD

Printed by Inprint + Design, University of Bradford
Cover design and setting: Chris Rowbottom

ISBN 978-0-9558400-3-6

ACKNOWLEDGEMENTS

All the poems in the 'Mosque' section were produced during projects in West Central Halifax for Chol Theatre and Heads (Participatory Arts in Calderdale), with the Square Chapel Arts Centre and Calderdale Dil Group. **8.30 am, most days; A large Qur'an** and **The Minbar of Sultan Qa'itbay** were included in *Sama Ghazal Salaam UK*, the 2009 collection of Persian, Arabic, Islamic and UK inspired poetry, edited by Chris Firth and published by Electraglade/Shutter Books. Extracts from **The Silver Jeweller, Sudden and unexpected** and **Blowing a sorrowful trumpet** were included in the film *Burlington Dreams*, commissioned by Integreat Yorkshire and funded by Yorkshire Forward for the MBED Partnership Skills Programme with Bridlington Renaissance. **The Silver Jeweller** and **I went into The Commercial** have been published in Cadaverine Magazine web.mac.com/thecadaverine/Site/ **He places his find in the rock cabinet** was a runner up in the 2010 East Riding Poetry Competition. **Against the Undercliff** is included in *Island Voices*, the 2010 anthology published by the Isle of Wight Poetry Society Stanza group. **Moor** and **Poetry when the sun stops** were commissioned as part of a tenure as Poet in Residence at the Ilkley Literature Festival in 2005 – **Moor** is also included in the electronic book, *Out of Ilkley*, edited by Antony Dunn and published for the 2010 festival; **Poetry when the suns stops** was published in *Praesepe*, the 2006 Beehive Poets anthology. **Three standing stones, A Hackney mother sends a parcel to Norfolk, Slave, History woman, A Zimbabwean in exile, Dr. Martin Kapel writes to Herold, That'll be the day** and **Two girls have birthdays** are included in the *Double Portraits* sequence commissioned by Kirklees Museums and Galleries to accompany the exhibition *6 Million+*. **Slave** was also published in the programme for *Food for Thought*, Kirklees' 2010 commemoration of Holocaust Memorial Day, in memory of John Chillag. **We pass his birthplace** was published in *Pennine Platform* and, with a Swedish translation, is included in poet Ralf Andtbacka's section on the Bröstoner site www.svof.fi/forfattare - Bröstoner is a project supporting Ostrobothnian Swedish language literature. **Drawing Oradour** was commissioned for the Kirklees commemoration of Holocaust Memorial Day in 2009. **My mother wallowed in the warmth** was written for a reading at Leigh and Wigan Words Together Literary Festival. **Kissi kaam ka nahin** was published on www.poetryunderthearches.blogspot.com.

CONTENTS

Fire

Feather

What comes from the lips
reaches the ear
What comes from the heart
reaches the heart

Arab proverb

Mosque

8.30 am, most days

In People's Park we walk and breathe, kamiz concealed
in anoraks to trounce the rain, earth under us.

And as we walk we climb again, hike mountain tracks
that browed our childhood years with snow, earth under us.

We walk around the broken glass, swish past the war,
conceive the English love for lines, earth under us.

Our stiff mill knees begin to ease, and yet we grieve
when weeds in chimneys catch the breeze, earth under us.

A circuit walked, we start again, move up a gear
to cheek this morning's sullen wheeze, earth under us.

Hydrangeas blue and pink our walk, explode the wash
and wet of green we've learnt to breathe, earth under us.

We walk among ourselves in hush, and long for heat
to dry this plush of blooms and leaves, earth under us.

O let us walk and breathe, breathe and walk, earth under us,
before Allah rolls up our rugs of time, earth over us,
earth under us, earth under us, earth over us.

A large Qur'an

(similar to work done at Shiraz, Iran, in the 1370s)

We stand among the lustre of tiles,
adjust to the dim, cloister light
as if waiting for the stretch of bats
behind glass in the nocturnal house.

I ask my friends, some in jackets,
some in kurtas, all hushed by ornament,
to name their most beautiful,
their Sesame of gold, crystal, silk.

I ask, though I know the answer.
One stall in this priceless bazaar draws all:
a cursive monument of ink and gilt
whose frozen rhythm demands breath.

This crack of lightning shook Arabia.
It's *Doctor Everything, voyage, mooring,*
the bride behind the veil, the deepest well,
the beginning and the endless.

My friends were once half faithful boys
who struggled with the dots and swirls
of compassionate and merciful syllables
as the mullah droned out the summer.

Now, their cock crow is grandchildren.
They know the Qur'an cleans hearts,
dips starlings in iridescent glaze,
reveals the star maps of faith.

In Gladstone Street, Rhodes Street,
five times a day they pray, wake
the desert sounds, illuminate
the hour, find light in their mouths.

The Minbar of Sultan Qa'itbay
(made in the period 1468 – 96)

Spangled with stars, as high as an oak tree,
inlaid with elephants' tusk, this radiant pulpit
preaches geometry, how everything intersects
in the mightiness of the Word, how the foci
of converging lines, the evenness of spaces
show a gifted promise, a yesness of meaning.

Imagine it beyond the slats of the city souk
in downtown Cairo, where the squelched
pink of over-ripe guavas stenches September
and sheep stew in fiery cauldrons big as rooms.

Wash up, enter, bow down, pray, leave pride
and meat smoke at the door, face the mihrab;
watch the imam approach the minbar's arch.
He opens two leaves, climbs heavenwards,
inhabits the heart-wood of the one craftsman
who hid his hand in exactness of repetition.

In mill town mosques with window bars,
bass boom and punches are left outside.
Two stone steps suggest such a minbar:
men bow down, praise God's geometry.

Mr. Sunny

Suraj, my name, once sown in sweet corn heat, means 'sun',
a proper Yorkshireman, a good Kashmiri son.

With battered book in hand, back home from school I'd run
to drive the oxen, a ploughboy berried brown by sun.

And then this foreign home – unspoken rules: keep mum,
don't answer back, sweep dust and never see the sun.

In just a year, I gained a weaver's rapid thumb
and learnt this awkward tongue in bone-tired daytime sun.

I taught my friends our new home's words and spread my sun
among their bread bun roti, cool Bismillah sons.

By selling door to door in wind-blown streets, I've done
what we all hoped: grown shops and vans in English sun.

Now retired, I phone around and sort out everyone,
advise a bit of 'when in Rome' in different sun.

So why do some see hidden bombs and rattling gun
when this Halifax man roams the streets in showery sun?

If others ask what's in your homespun heart, Suraj,
don't speak of heavy rain; uncloud the sun.

Tile with a diagram of the
Noble Sanctuary in Mecca
(Turkey, probably Iznik, 17th century)

Pilgrims' tales, that's what the men want to tell,
as they cluster round this chunk of quartz-paste:
a glazed map of territory they know better
than their backyards, fire daily in their hearts.

The hardest pillar

On one of those bucket-down, stay in,
light the gas fire, put on a jumper days
when rivers of rain slop down the streets,
the would be Hajjis pack their bags
and set off on the short sky road to Mecca.

With the first shudder of turbulence,
they know they're somehow different,
carried by a winged, inevitable wind
to a black rock rising, a draped truth
they frame in gold on sitting room walls.

*

Concrete simmers, taxis bubble over,
whole cities queue for taps, lips crackle.
The vastness of arrival heaves forward,
switches off a million phones, catches
heat waves, becomes white lava.

The unstoppable flow of mumbled prayers
bottle-necks when it meets the destination.
Even the hardest, most stubborn stones,
trapped in the flow, crack as they tumble
against the forgiving block of the Ka'ba.

*

The Hajjis return home, forget crush, flies,
battle with fog, sleet and unreliable cars.
Life's sometimes grim. Hearts softened,
brothers rebreathe peace, cling to the rock.

Shah Tahmsap I and his sword
(Iran, 1524 – 76)

A miniaturist, an executioner
who loved flowers and filigree.

I was just ten when my father died,
mewling, surrounded by wine skins.
The tribal chiefs kept me on strings
till I was old enough to comb my beard.

A painter of banquets, a torturer
who made calligraphers court officials.

Five times we drove back the Uzbeks.
I learnt to sever heads quick enough:
brothers, ministers, the prancing hordes
who kicked our doors in, bladed our children.

A connoisseur of eye colours, a seducer
who petted a zoo of women.

We were always on the move.
You can't carry palaces on camels
so art gave some constancy,
tinted the burnt grain gold again.

A designer of hunting carpets, a despot
who studied the intricacies of snares.

I had a sword made
in a short season of rain.

The charcoal in the forge
shone like blood-oranges.

The smith's sweat sizzled
on the fiery curve
like the last buzz of flies
dropped into a candle flame.

Daytrip to Rydal Water

Heaven promised

this Sunday morning, when we packed the minibus,
and counted topied heads while someone's mother
slid from a black estate in the mosque yard,
her coffin cloth resplendent with yellow *ayah*.

Heaven expected

on the journey there, passing car boot sales,
oil-puddled truck stops, sheep like peeled turnips
strewn on threadbare hillocks, Gothic B&Bs
and the Urdu-ness of the word *Gymkhana*.

Heaven

when we emerged into filmy Lakeland
and the cracked patience of walls without cement,
when we scaled small mountains in sandals
and downed bottled water in the bracken.

Heaven

in fir tree pillars of green darkness;
in the meticulous crossing of stepping stones,
a progress with umbrellas and handholds
into the serene gloom of the slate cave.

Heaven fulfilled

we pose like proud goats for the group photo,
secure in the Kashmir-ness of this landscape,
quietly Bollywood, before we take the coffin route
on the east side of the water, struggling with
repaired arteries and *yadasht*, our memory
of promise, and how we found the longest walk.

Note: *ayah* are verses from the Qur'an

Stone

The silver jeweller

For Carlo Giovanni Verda

On a day of frozen fog, rime frost:
every tree, every hedge dipped silver-white
like the ammonite you cast from the beach –
lucky find become holy shine –
you expound on body, mind and soul,
keeping the soul for your own territory:
the liminal, between thought and hand,
reckoned and sensory, like your tradition –
seolfer-smith, 'he who seethes silver by fire',
he who pins, solders, buffs the crystalline
into clasps and brooches of sailing ships

like the shallow draft, clinker-built vessel
of Sutton Hoo, resting place and treasure hoard
of Raedwald of the dynasty of Beowulf,
cyninga, 'king', owner of Byzantine silver
wave-rocked on a high bluff in Suffolk
among his christening spoons and spears.

Aeons after you cross the sea to the next world
you hope to be disinterred with your talismans:
white boats, delicate hammers and lustrous fossils
signifying a man of influence; beneficent, ideaful,
'he who talked well on the strand and was of some note,
gave some service', *cyninga*, king in the Saxon sense

meaning the child, not the father, of his people;
the summit of his class, who lived long and well
in a street of makers and thinkers, who knew
the structure of silver contains the herring bone,
a fruit of the sea picked clean, winged and perfect.

He places his find in the rock cabinet

Joshua   home-schooled

adds   his cube stone

to plant furl stones   basalts and granite

two ammonites   from Jard-sur-Mare

and banded ironstone   two billion years old

before oxygen   before limbs fins rust

I watch him   and think back

to Half Moon quarry   on Foxcote Hill

my first find   my belemnite

I chipped the mollusc spire   from honey stone

rubbed it clean   weighed the sea in my palm

ocean arrow   sleek fossil

Devonian squid   cuttlefish cousin

perfect swimmer   from the Old Red Age

Joshua becomes   motionless

stone bound

Or mineral

Gneiss with Hornblende, Garnet, Mica, Schist,
toothy Amethyst, pressed sunset of Agate.

Ribboned Tourmaline: rhubarb laid in silver.
Green Chalcedony: pondweed trapped in ice.

Flirting stones delight with light.
Angles refract to the meditative.

The attendant wraps Peacock ore:
glitter of copper, purple, bronze.

Back home I dig into the dark bag,
tear paper, watch dazzle flip in air.

Human geology

We heard the knock on the door,
broke off our fight, half-met his eyes
when we saw his black-coated leanness.

He said the girl had fallen in the Parish Hall -
a game at Brownies, a chair, a fall.
As a churchgoer, would I bear the coffin?

So I slow stepped in the drizzle
and her family glided in a haze
before we laid her down in the landscape.

The Penwith sun painted no warmth.
A hound cry of fog shrouded the Tor.
Her family touched without words.

Later that week, we walked out
to Mên-an-Tol, 'stone with a hole';
an eerie piercing, a burial entrance.

We'd read the spells: three times naked
through the belted air toward the sun
to cure a child's brittle bones.

We knelt down on either side:
our rite was a snatched kiss
bounded by a circle, to heal the rift.

That casual prayer was a removal of stone,
a carving out on the pale, spacey moor;
our seer's gaze through to quiet love

knowing we all sift down,
suddenly become the memory
of few people for a short time.

Three standing stones

At six you might have sung geese -
Goosy goosy gander, whither, wander
though your words included v and z.

I sung lasses and lads leaving their dads
who trip it trip it to the maypole high:
every he gets a she, every she a he.

Like you I enjoyed long walks with my father.
He did not take me to the Tatra Mountains
but to long barrows and standing stones.

We passed the exams for Grammar School.
I went. You didn't. You tore up their twisted crosses.
Black eagles nested and the storm surged in.

You were blown to a distant city of steel,
became Cinderella in a drawing office.
She got her he at fifteen, borrowed a frock.

A golden egg: the pure joy of your first child.
At the crossroads, you took the owl's path.
The Queen garlanded you with honours.

My father told me some standing stones
are knights, frozen under a witch's spell,
their story stopped for ever:

your mother and father
your Grammar School
your words with 'v's and 'z's

Against the Undercliff

The island: downs, chines, Needles.
Where he can always swim in the sea.
This is the third time, healing the second:
Quorn cutlets, flooded room, *I'm leaving you.*
They sleep under the thatch; things have changed.
She lets him not unpack his bags, strokes his hair.

She's in bed while he leans out, catches the secret:
badgers speed around the lawn like wind-ups,
lap the Greekish fountain and snaffle
the leftovers of salmon béarnaise, Paris Brest.
Five foxes, heads low, one with a snagged brush,
footpad the borders. The flick of small bats.

Next day, the rainy forest, a red squirrel safari;
graffiti on the hide: nosquirrels.com
Back to the beach: the pile driver, the last day
of school. Leavers wade into the waves
in skirts, white shirts, push each other under.
She moves her deckchair closer.

Farringford. Left alone in Tennyson's study,
they can almost scent his smoking cap.
They stand at the top of the spiral staircase
where he escaped from the heaviness of family.

Even cliffs give way. This week's headline:
Sunbather nearly crushed by cow.

Unfriended creatures

The opening of Cornelia Parker's
'Brontëan Abstracts'
at Haworth Parsonage.

Those sisters kept wildness between lines,
blotted carefully, quill-scratched on
while everything closed in, closed down.

Hair strands, tweezered from lockets,
have been forensically magnified:
Charlotte's kemptness, Emily's split ends.

Comb teeth have become severed fingers.
As we raise a toast to the cleverness of art,
bus shelter hoots cut the quiet.

Hero and heroine tear up the lace:
two ASBO kids jump on graves
and try each other out with tongues

the other side of the wall. Someone is sent.
This is by invitation – no room for Cathy
and the Gypsy brat with their shared fag

making for the moor: slackers
who should learn to show respect
and how to curl their 'f's and 'g's.

They kiss-chase around the stones,
then give us the finger, scramble
through a gap, blow away into the heather.

We're uneasily drawn back
to giant scans of Charlotte's pincushion
and Emily's imperfect stocking darns.

A wild wick slip she was
and much too fond of Heathcliff.

Sun spotlights the church clock.
Rooks crackle in the sudden nip of dusk.

Moor

Off the motorway – spray, flatbacks,
tiredness can kill – to wrap himself
in rocks, hear holes, sip ironwash.

He climbs to the knoll, views cattle,
distantly neat; watches tiny moths
mob heather; carries on up and up

until he loses houses, finds flatness,
leans into the rainwind, soothed
by the stretch of sky, the absences.

Sudden and unexpected

For Penelope Weston

An absence made present: his Anglican-ness,
his books – *The Food of Love, The Rule of Taizé* –
library this new old house for friends who stay
to share your days of quiet and busyness.

So not the sort to dwell on emptiness,
with Frank not doing it, you learned to pray
and planted gourds and salvia to slay
the demon grief and find a different fullness.

And then the sculpture angle-ground in stone –
a garden 'Hug' for him, for everyone,
enormous lump of universal love.

Historic rooms become an office-home,
your crumbling High Street hub where you've undone
the shock, pricked out the seedling, grow alone.

On Orkos beach

Between the crowds and no-one
we count pebbles, find balances.

Slowly and separately, we make
our names: small blacks on white.

You tear fallen leaves, puzzle a heart.
I build towers that are always falling.

As you sleep, I stack two pillars
and bridge them with a capstone
heavy as a bucket of sea.

On top, I teeter a spire of shingle
and weathercock it with an unripe olive.

The shadows drop like anchors
to monument this frippery.

When you wake, we huddle on a log,
contemplate our Karnak, our Parthenon.

Lay

The second island week. A mad-dog walk
in Paxos heat from beach to Circe's spring.
My bottle's dry when I arrive and climb
the bell tower steps, spot you, flat out and dozing.
You're scaly, not spry enough to paw the breasts
of Nausicaa's oily maids, though you drowse-sigh
their high vowels. I think 'Poor old Homer'
and leave you there, epic'd-out, a snoring line.

Once the sea floor

Out of glacier scour and melt
rose this wedge of an island,
a riverless sieve
of pocks and holes;
a water joke, waterless;
a dry deck
in a salty bliss of sea.

The ancestors dug deep,
only to drop sweat beads
in brackish puddles.

At night, they ate gritty bread,
drank sour wine
and swore at stories
of water nymphs.

They toiled chisel years
in the netherworld
for their grandchildren,
hollowed out *sterna*,
giant pits necked like bottles

cave tanks to catch
the winter rains

black pitchers
cupped
by fossil rock:
molluscs, corals,
sponges, soft claws.

Under each flagstone lid,
they carved an eye
to wet-shine
when they lifted the weight
after the first storms.

They knew the value
of the glyph:
the sight-lift
towards clouds
after drought.

They terraced
the rattle slopes

rammed spade blunting earth
between
labyrinths of walls
ploughed
                    planted.

The women trudged summers,
inked prints of jars
on their heads.

Olive shoots grew
slower than lifespan.

The grandchildren shook down
shoals of hard fruit,
pressed them
between wheelstones.

Then runnels ran with green ooze
squeezed through mats
until the slithery oil glittered.

They built archways
to their houses
and began to tell tales
of long haired girls
who rise out of the sea,
walk up the shore,
run through thorns,
bleed rainwater.

Country

Sea Squill

Late August, walking inland
past cockerels and yucca,
I nearly crush delicate monsters.

They thrust upwards
like vegetable jokes:
bawdy steeples
broached with white stars.

Blizzard catch
hung from limp verticals,
pewter-lilac stalks
sprung up
from rusty soccer balls –

Homer's sea onions
tooled up
to survive forest fires
or twenty years on a shelf.

Once named after Scilla,
the disturber – a goddess
famous for her tsunami howls.

The locals eased the bulbs
from between the stones,
baked, sliced, boiled
until the syrup stenched
their hearths:
cough mixture, bowel loosener.

Imagine the taste:
a mix of tears and dust.

They hung these ragged planets
over doors at New Year's Eve
and delved for babies
in the winter wrap-around.

Rigani (Greek oregano)

Where mountains slide into sea
and they brew urns of chamomile,
boil quince, spoon dollops of sour cherry,
in the almost siesta shade of the grocer's
I crush crisp florets between finger and thumb,
unloose a stony gasp of aromatic dust:
whiff of bridal garlands, skin on skin,
white blooms of June, peaceful tombs.

Back home its paler relative, tucked in gabions,
prodded in troughs, flowers later but still speaks
of hives on the scree, goat stews, ovens in lean-tos.

Odysseus' scarlet sails waft to the next island.
His Ithacans dunk their dry bread in the first press
spiced with sear *rigani*.
                              The sun's gates open wide.

For John

Not sheep's heads boiled by your mother
or the effortless arc of your bowling arm

Not buttered crusts in dour kitchen light
or the untimely cut of your long shorts

Not warm eggs and the scatter of hens
or your sombre cementing with your father

Not the charcoal of Cub camp sausages
or freckles on your see-through hands

 But your full larder knowledge
of our boyhood land-roves

the repose in your swift change
of my tail light bulb

your precise naming
of each field edge tractor wreck

the weighty prose
of digging me up after so many years

the unbearable fact of nothing
and everything in common

the much too soon lost
ease of your companionship.

I tell a boy's tale

one begun long ago in Wayfinder shoes
at the door of a mucked up farm
where I am asking for half a dozen eggs.

The ruddy balloon-like woman takes my change,
lets her brown hens scrit around the yard
and her sons scoop pickles from the floor.
My mother waits for eggs and cheese and me.

I can always find that morning
and wish my words would yolk the page
that clouty yellow I've never met again.

Sometimes it's easier to write about eggs
with the colour of largeness and freedom
than the way touch changes over time.
I could write about how we both talk to ourselves
or the long haired baby who is your great grand-daughter
or why, after so long, you miss the natter of the village

but in this tale you still tuck me in at night
and read me a story of tiny people
with borrowed names, like Homily and Pod.

I can see you, mother. I can see me.
I can see snow falling on Middle Street
and Lady Flower walking her poodles.
If you crack this tale open, you'll find love
inside shells thick with mud and straw.
And eggs to coddle, scramble, sizzle, poach.

I went into The Commercial

I went into The Commercial
in Slaithwaite, West Yorkshire.
And slowly downed a pint of cider
                        tasting of childhood –
the giant barrel next to the coal shed
where I kept a rock hammer
                        hung on a nail.

My hemp bag was full of paper, books –
that one about the peregrine which begins
with a long ridge like the hull of a submarine
and flies through a shredded sky.

The pub had been upgraded, wine-barred.
Bellies and baldies had moved on,
found a home up the hill at The Shoulder.

But a trio hung on like a grim documentary.
A local cowboy, denimed and sideboarded,
babbled of stolen goods and 'What will my mum do?'
to a couple who sat like individual puddings.

I read, my head clouded and I left,
ducking under the railway bridge
beneath leaves speed-pressed to Teflon
on the sleek slowworm silver of the rails.

Out in the wet wet night, I thought
'How did I end up here?' under tough stars
at the beginning of another winter.

I grew up in mellow hills,
pressed in the folds of the Midlands –
lovely thatch, that grass snake on the cut trunk;
hawthorn, blackthorn and elm in the hedge.

Why did I ever come north?
Graffiti on dripping walls, fog in the throat

a way to nothing

like the sliver paths between the heather
trudging up to a glowing, one-hawked sky.

Christmas morning

Before I fluffed the roast potatoes, I looked
outside, tasted the frost. Mysterious night!
Violas tippled from the tub, hooves on ice
clued by teardrop droppings (we checked the book).
A bus stop rumour of one among the sheep,
a dog walker who glimpsed shy contours.
Now wildness had stood by our kitchen door
and moved on while we dreamt story, asleep.

In this mill hamlet, above the urban straggle
of chemical process, imprisoned chickens,
we do not expect great light, angels, an agile
roe deer broken free from wintry fiction.
Seas rise, land mammals fade away;
we touched the deepest world today.

Tree lines
Thomas Pitfield, 1903 – 1999

Last walks in Dunham Park, your sight thin strings –
far mist of Fallow herd; gnarled bole
close enough for touch. You bend down and roll
your fingertip back and forth, count annual rings,
look back on ninety-six: that long sing
of notes and art that grew from the folderol
of a toy stage to the fine control
of a flute sonatina, a tender carving of wings.

Your many talents served a long fibred creed:
Peace be to the people through engraved rain
and the compressed music of a January wood.

You knew how to stand in the presence of leaves:
this softened marks cut across the grain
as you worked the tree for the common good.

Too small, too torn

I

My fourteenth summer. Dad wakes me up
before the squabble of birds; the fruit mice
are stripping the trees. I pull on my trainers,
lick my hand and pat my hair. He doesn't speak,
brushes hay from his Sunday coat,
then leads the way to town.

Dad strides in front, a fug of hurry.
He'd met these men, all dressed in shiny black,
came back full of it, told me to pack my bag.
At first I cried, and then began to spend
on lipstick, heels, a loaf of currant bread.

We reach the square; the big important man is here,
his van a squash for six of us; potato sacks,
tomato crates. We haven't met but squeal
when thrown together by the bumps.

A long rattling
and the clouds roll over the moon.

II

Once upon a time, I arrived in a country.

My fourteenth summer. Tomasz wakes me up,
calls me 'little chit', says: 'This is what you do
my cockatoo, my plumling, bitch.'
And then he did a dirty thing. At first I cried.

A long rocking
and the clouds roll over the moon.

III

Once upon a time, I arrived in your country.

'Slip-slops' he calls them, these feathered boats.
He won't give us outdoor shoes.
I feel I'm painted on a wall when,
on hands and knees, I eat the floor.
Film star, pop star, wife and priest.
Bad girl, schoolgirl, gypsy, thief.

Out there, the trees blow over
and the clouds swallow the moon.

A Hackney mother sends a parcel to Norfolk, 1939

I wrapped the contents (brothers, small, x 2)
in a bagel bag (it was all I had), tucked in
my sweet shrunken sons, tied it
with pudding string, sealed it
with candle wax left from Shabbat.

They squeaked inside like larder mice
but fell quiet when their teacher called by
in his muffled brogues to pick them up.
He curled his hand under the string,
boarded a bus, set off for the country.

At the first door, he pulled the bell.
A maid came, flustered between courses,
got a sudden whiff of dank, rank child.
'You could try down the lane', she said.
By the third village, despair had set in.

What hurt most was the ballet slippers
of a girl who clutched her mother's apron
when the oily scent seeped across the mat.
'Not for me', she said. 'I want a pretty thing
not cranky beggar dolls who'll tug my plaits.'

By the fifth, the teacher was on his knees.
He thought they'd have to sleep in the hedge
until a woman wide as a bull said, 'I'll take 'em.'
She went to stuff them under the eaves,
hoping they'd keep out the rain and swell up.

She stirred pigs' heads, made basins of brawn.
'Don't you like a bit of crackling, a bit of belly, tinies?'
Her eldest lad dangled them under the yard tap.
They walked to school in darkness, came back
in darkness, bruised by desk lids, pinched slate blue.

In bed by seven, they shivered under holey sheets.
The lardy family warmed their chubby joints
around the grate and hockled dialect words
for 'vermin, midgets, lumber', spat on coals.
They wrote, 'Please mum, come and take us away.'

I went to that country pancake of a farmhouse.
I said nothing, looked into her gorgon eyes.
My sons were even smaller. I hugged them
in the parcel of my hands, took them back
to daylight bombs. They grew, grew large as boys.

Blowing a sorrowful trumpet

The first sorrow of the blacksmith
is the steel twists
of a helter-skelter beyond the coastguard station -
hard labour of long hours
lashed by soaked wind on the North Shore,
fenced in, childless.

The second sorrow
is the doubting Thomas at Walkington Hayride
who didn't believe he'd completely rebuilt
the fourteen seater horse-drawn charabanc,
didn't trust his lineage –
a big family who could do it all.

And the third sorrow
is a passing of names:
naff, fellies – elm hub and ash rim of the wheel.
Proud trades bend and break
in the weather of a fast time;
churchyard crocuses in snow.

The fourth sorrow
is the pizzicato twitter of his daughter's viola,
available for download and London concert hall.
He hammers her separateness
on the face of his grandfather's anvil;
she returns each Christmas.

The fifth sorrow
is a breaking up of the camp –
wife and self-made house, who left together.
These days he doesn't light the forge:
there are holes in the hood
and fourteen hours a day is not enough.

The sixth sorrow
is a perceived threat –
the old families who live in the Old Town
shoved out by new money and apartments,
connections sundered for ever;
grubbed out oaks, sawn up for firewood.

And the last sorrow
is himself –
a clever man who could have chosen another way,
flown above the clouds with the RAF,
retired to a Mediterranean beach
if it hadn't been for his iron persistence
and the deft undertow of tradition.

The Irish Nanny

The Alfa Romeo drove like a slow cigarette,
a lipstick drag round hairpin bends,
stubbed out on arrival at the starlit villa.

They gave her Vogue twins, thought she'd know
what to do, how to dab their waxy folds.
She soon tied nappies quicker than hair bows.

Iron-bedded in a gap between dog chains,
vinegar wine and powdery olive boughs,
she slept fitfully, pricked by straw.

They let her out. Beyond the gate groan
all was bright gouache: paste of pink mortar,
carmine splat of flower heads, whole tube of sky.

He leant against the lorry, and when his teeth
broke the skin of that beach ball tomato -
pomodoro, 'golden apple' – she found her hero.

He would rescue her from suds and bugs.
She gushed a burble of 'l's and 'm's
streaked with the watery vowels of Antrim.

When he loped towards her, wiping his chin,
she ascended a leaning tower, sailed in a gondola,
stood breathlessly on that Verona balcony.

The murk and mess vanished into the heavy air.
She'd never love the country but would love him forever:
the crack on her face of his chilli breath,

his foul-mouthed hands, the joy of something to confess,
her sudden heat in the basement
like a dizzy woodlouse, stone trapped, running in dark.

Legends

We followed the Shannon, sponged up
the sideways rain for a week
after the Scriptorium of Clonmacnoise
where we'd seen the crack of the spread legged Mother.
She peed down on us all the way to Limerick,
cackling, *Ah you boys, you dirty English boys.*

Often, we didn't see a hire cruiser for hours.
To be sure it was a quest for the marvellous,
pitching our tent on the floating grass,
glad of soggy cornflakes, glad of soggy everything
until the sky finally married the river
and the cows grew fins.

We arrived too early at the dripping hostel,
soaked to a standstill.
Cast up among the ting ting creak of metal beds,
we were terrorised by the snoring of Vikings
and longed for Brian Boru
to throw them out into the street.

Next day, we drowned in pints of the Murphy's
and took a vow to give up this canvas life.

Brother Wildlife

My filmmaker brother's back in the country,
takes me for a forced march up the valley,
struts his jungle legs, picks blackberries
without stopping.

He lives in landscapes,
aeroplanes from one to the other,
rescues gibbons,
puts sticks in crocodiles' mouths,
follows tribal bum-cracks up mountain tracks,
risks malaria and melanoma.

We're soon out on the moor.
Though each trefoil of clover holds water,
summer's dried out the peat crust.
We look down on the golf course.
Scourges, environmental vandalism.
They're breeding, all over the world.

He's angry about so much:
the cult of David Attenborough,
Americans, America, colour filters,
blood dripping out of suitcases.

He's amazed at the heather this year,
the sharp line between sky and land
and pinches the glands of the lemon scented fern.
If we could just get rid of human beings.

He enthuses about smoking sheds,
the black net lofts of Hastings;
how to cook mackerel
with blackberry and apple;
what a superb series he will make
and how it will sell worldwide.

We pass his birthplace

For Ralf Andtbacka

Öde: abandoned, fate. Lost in the boglands.
Hours driving the straight road, hoping for an elk
until the trees close. Guessing at pine tar black:
talons, sleeping barns, fur farms.

He recognises the void. *Someone's at home.*
My brother married a girl from the town.
Sometimes, we pulled animals into our world.
All the dogs died and were buried side by side.

His pastoral is shut up for the night.
Light lives, gusting away. A few cows,
a bit of logging and worry, like horse ticks,
burrowing into rafter contentment.

His countrymen name potatoes after girls.
There is a lot of time for quietness
among the livestock. Pools green with moss
where writers and farmers lie side by side.

Fire

Finlanders

Hemman: a homestead, dimly lit by candles and oil,
packed with crooked doorways and seats from sleighs.
His ancient hosts had lit a birch fire and cut rye bread.

Like ice melt, they creak in the hollows of their bunk,
this worn, quaffing couple who tell life through wars.
She has undone her silver clasp, her lace collar,
her tweed suit of forest blue; he's digesting Karelian stew.

Their visitor stares up at the bow and sag,
traces the curlicues of carved love spindles
and takes an angel's head from under the bed.

On the day she found it, she blew its gold out of dust.
He came down from patching the roof to see
and she bellowed the stove, brewed Russian tea
before he ferried her on his handlebars to the sea.

She breaks the surface with her blonde hair,
calls to her young husband on the fling of mud.
It's all beginning; they believe writing changes things.

Slag: punch, knock, battle. Something lived through;
how they had to learn German, came to English too late,
how the stag's head squinnies at the window view,
startled by the petrol station's fluorescent glow.

My mother wallowed in the warmth

For a girl who'd never travelled north,
Leigh was the cacti house, flowered
with mine wheels and clocks of cotton fluff,
tended by thumps of men, clogged up,
smutted by underground and chimneystacks;
the same gods – Winston and Jesus;
something like the same language
but stove-warmed, deeper, briefer.

She'd arrived after an endless train journey
still in the stale crispness of her uniform,
carrying a Bible inscribed with her address.
She'd been puzzled, and moved, by the welcome:
the cheers of a town lifting the station roof.
This wasn't America (promised in the Blitz)
but far enough from the darts of silver birds
who soared over an edgy Kingston afternoon.

They'd spent a mattress night in the Town Hall.
before the queue rolled up in the morning,
eager to house the hundred, take their pick.
A hanger for baby clothes waited in a bedroom:
the Cable Works Manager and his wife
had not expected two shorthand students
whose white buckskin shoes came in black
after their first paddle in the coal mud.

Used to whale, powdered egg, half portions,
they thrived on the heaviness of dumplings;
extra helpings excused the lack of a cruet.
They grew sturdy with weekend hikes
up Rivington Pike, beat away the mist wraiths
and bussed back to streets where the houses,
shored up and patched with iron plates,
contemplated collapse, like teetering rhinos.

In '45, back in the torn flatness of London,
she cried at buried stories, grew lighter,
missed the strikes of 'Hello lass' on the street.

*

Going north to greet her first grandchild,
she makes a detour but can't spot the big mine.
The view's too horizontal, too clean.

She unfolds chimneys, pegs them to the sky,
scatters soot petals on concrete drives.
Finding the cul-de-sac, the semi-detached,
she hangs her heart (and her blue velour hat)
on the peg, smells hot beetroot, potato pie,
loosens her striped tie, tucks into grace.

Drawing Oradour

For Robert Perry

You can't ink the wind-whine in tram wires,
theme for these steps to nowhere, spook-lit
by paraffin lamp: stone witness to fires
that razed the town, left only things to speak.
You can't draw the people of this backwater
but hear their voices in the night-creak:
'We sang under deep green cradles. Resist?
A little. But to melt bells, heap up slaughter?'

That morning, a woman dashed up this stairway,
clumped across the lost floor and found a leather
satchel for her son. By six, they both gazed
blank in the church, piled in the sultry weather.
Shot in the legs, the men died in the barn blazes.
Black liquid corners, and loss that lasts for ever.

Slave

John Chillag, a Hungarian Jew at Bochum Verein KZ,
August 1944 – March 1945

Numbered

not shipped, not whipped (though some were).
Hit and thumped by German foremen,
fed on potato peel, thin as sheet steel
you forged gun barrels thicker than oaks.

Young

not broken, not smoke (though most soon were),
you sweated below the presses, Hans above.
You hatched a scheme: he'd lower the hoist,
crush your toes. Plaster: no roll call, no work.

Survivor

unlike Hans, unlike your father, unlike most.
Forty years to forge the unspeakable.
Then you raise the hoist, stop the press,
lift out the white hot rods.

History woman
Irena Basarab, born 23 March 1922

Your straw hat shadows your face
- a creased map of unstable names.
You fettle stories of stone lions, orators
and a wood crowned with a cloud
of Jewsmoke, including the tailor
your father paid in food. You shroud
your factory years in plain cotton,
embroider flowers on forgotten wars.

I want to label you: Ukrainian, historian,
mother, talker, blanket maker, mender.
This shrivels your world, the long harm
of exile, the tangled threads of Europe.

Kashya's tour

St. Nicholas' Eve, when presents are given
and birdsong struggles in the trees
behind the unchanged gunpowder factory.
We pay for our private guide at a window.

Kashya tells us her aerial came off in the car wash
and this is her first day driving on ice.
How she waits too long at junctions
and works seven days a week in summer.

How her best gift ever was a green play tent
and she spent all day in it with her sister.
How, despite the storks, she thinks Oswięçim ugly
and her home is far away in the south-west.

She tells us how the lights failed yesterday
and another guide got locked in one of the huts.
How he was fortunate to own a mobile phone;
that the car seat is her seven year old daughter's.

How Queen Sofia of Belgium paid for the toilets
in which the hand dryer does not work.
How, in the year Spielberg built huts in the fields,
there was no harvest and many new televisions.

She tells us there are families of foxes and one cat;
that Gypsy children had holes in their cheeks.
How some patent shoes are still in good condition.
How faces were covered with something like moss.

How this place was chosen because of railways,
that they are moving towards an exact number.
How she stayed up with her sister to see St. Mikołaj
and how the green tent flew away in summer.

Later we will find chocolates on our pillows
and slowly sip glasses of honey liqueur.
Kashya will boil pierogi from a packet
and read her daughter a story about a saint.

I tell her the windows on the bus were misted up
so we missed the camp but the driver went back;
that tomorrow we are going to the salt mines
and we live with our two daughters near Leeds.

I do not tell her about my brother-in-law
who still believes that facts are fiction.
How he binds books and had to kill his pigeons.
How easily he picked up the wrong ideas.

A Zimbabwean in exile writes to Herold, his eight year old son and companion

The worst time is night

                        I see her – your mother, my wife –
and wish for the time before unspeakable things, when my life
meant more than shirt and jeans hung on weightless bones
dumped in the chill of a borrowed room.

The worst time is night

                        I hold her – your mother, my wife –
my heart knows she's gone but my arms clutch her tight
in the baked shadows. Wildebeest gather, thatches burn,
blowflies lay eggs on the meat of our friends.

I dream her alive

                        when I see you – my son, my life –
my unexpected one who flew on a plane, ran from behind
to fall, like a half remembered photo, into my buckled hands,
smelling of harvest time, my other children, my wife.

I dream her alive

                        when I hold you – my son, my life.
You wake our wedding, the veldt, bare feet, the bright
gashed skies before violation of secret places, the night
running, the ashy questions you'll ask one day.

I dream her alive

                        hear seeds rattle in the gourd.

Dr. Martin Kapel writes to Herold

Notice normal things, like squirrels, post,
the careful way to paint a window frame,
a woman knitting, broken cars on trailers,
leaf fall, bus stops, cat doors, skips.

It took me years to see the normal things
after the trains, that march in the dark forest,
the way a child falls sideways into a ditch,
the greyness of Krakow, the crash of Coventry.

Sometimes at night my world unhinges
(this is a normal thing): I scrape for turnips
among the tarry dead, turn over my cousins.
But I've lived long, have my shirts pressed.

And you, Herold, who came this August:
I was the wardrobe myself, like you.
I too was eight, liked my English school,
adjusted, did well (I'm sure you will too).

Notice normal things, like those questions
you'll always be asked (you'll learn answers),
how no one will allow you to be normal,
how Krakow and Coventry are just cities.

That'll be the day

That tinny azaan,
a white slab of sunlight,
a stashing of bed rolls.

I put on the leather boots
they gave us the first day,
sneak pitta into my pocket.

I shoulder my gun.
Part of me is John Wayne:
draw   railroad   kinda.

It happens so quickly.
The kid has a gun.
He *draws*. I *draw*. Then

she runs round the corner.
One of my bullets *kinda*
splits open her bundle.

She drops the red rags.
I say a prayer before
she screams. Then run.

Jamal saw. 'Shit happens',
he says. 'She'll be proud,
bury it in their sun flag.'

Tomorrow the azaan,
the white slab of sunlight,
the stashing of bed rolls.

Soon I'll eat tabbouleh.
I'll remember how a gun
once made me happy.

Poetry when the sun stops

On attending a reading by Mario Petrucci, author of 'Heavy Water'.

By candles and gas mantles – such small lights –
we assemble: the lady with bunches, the journalist
in shorts who knee-worships this longest night,
teachers, a late mother, a turbaned poet, a pissed
plumber who's stumbled in on a scene by Rembrandt –
yellow glow; leather sagged faces with raven stares;
clamped hands heavy as car springs; a resonant
attentive hush brought on by your flare
for clarity, for holding up to the sun lies and lives,
the meltdown of Chernobyl: a three tailed fox, bones
soft as white sea urchins. Foam drenches a bride;
shoes melt, and feet; a daughter buries an accordion.

Energy is all around. Why go faster than we need?
No one wets their lips. We're stuck in that cold
dark, twenty years ago. Glistening acres of seeds
await gatherers in spacesuits. We will grow old,
most of us. Outside, shadows unload sacks
of onions from the back of a van. The moon's
a greying grandpa spat at by stars. Cracks
in the concrete open. Dead villagers play tunes.

The skaters

The year before pack and helmet, you're still a boy.

The scene is windless – your icy smallness
dabbed on the field's edge beyond the brickworks.
You tie blades to your boots, slip-stamp,
whoop to your mates, bones poised
for the long skate from Peterborough to the sea

When they have to shoot the horses, you're still a boy.

The scene is greyed out – your chest full of air,
your lousy smallness furiously pedalling;
a mud-caked messenger on a black bike
flying up the line from Albert to Amiens,
keeping flat at night – toothed fish in the ice.

When the fields are finished, you're still alive.

The scene is almost unlit – on the London Road
your bowed head remembers the long skate;
how the cloud wisps were sparrow hawk feathers
when you sped free, trousers frozen to the knee
while inside you blazed and crackled like a brazier.

When they sent out six hundred, two came back.

The scene shifts to the rest of a long lifetime.
When you marry the tall girl, you are already numb,
up to your thighs in mud, whether pointing walls,
singing of the immortal and invisible
or striking your son for not being there.

Your grandsons' questions ricochet off your plating.

Each night, in no-man's-land, you try to find the skaters.
The scene is striped by phosphor flashes:
that bike in a tangled heap, wire rips in your sleeves.
No shine on the fen; ice gone, land drained,
a crop of boots sprung up like wheat.

Feather

Two girls have birthdays

Ibi, 1938, Tokaj, Hungary.

You are fourteen. You can see

your father singing scripture
by the synagogue's blue ark

armfuls of apples, rowed
from the other side of the river

a girl quick with her hands
who plans to study haute couture.

You are fourteen. You cannot see

two narrow slits
which snap air and light
into a musky wagon

a city of chicken coops
where nothing grows,
not even horseradish

a soaked lunatic
who stands in the dark,
waiting to be counted.

Zenebu, 1974, Alamata, Ethiopia.

You are fourteen. You can see

a friend from Primary School
who brings coffee to her husband

your father, the detective,
reading Freud under the eucalyptus

'a really happy girl', who runs,
looks forward to libraries.

You are fourteen. You cannot see

the intricate eyes of a teacher
under a poster
sticky with blood

house watchers
who smoke at the roadside,
check no one mourns

yellow wagtails
flying over a room
where a woman hangs,
upside down.

Kissi kaam ka nahin (of absolutely no worth)

Beside a rusting tower a boy plays.
He kicks a football before a sudden fall.
It could be somewhere here – Teeside or the greys
of Ellesmere Port – girders, a flaking city
of tubes and funnels, holding tanks, skulls
sprayed on a wall and a roost of shabby birds.

They say on that night even passing birds
dropped from the sky, but a boy still plays
where cows' eyes bubbled in splitting skulls.
They say thousands died in their sleep before the fall
of ash dimmed the daylight of the city
where row after row was laid under blanket greys.

Now, in the evening reds and morning greys
tangles of bushes and wire echo with birds.
The flare site still taunts this lake city
where a mother pumps water and a boy plays
among leaking drums before a sudden fall
and a football that rolls away in a place of skulls.

They say on that night the delicate skulls
of babies glowed like streetlamps, the mud greys
of shanty floors were stained red by the fall
of boiling blood while all the shrieking birds
fell silent as families' shrine displays
of flowered gods melted in the beloved city.

Twenty-six years later a mother of this city
walks through a hole in a wall by furious skulls.
She grips her son's hand as he stubbornly plays
with a football dusted by the poisoned greys
of soil from beside a rusting tower where birds
nest and he's grazed his knee in a sudden fall.

They say on that night the leaf fall
from the street-worn trees was complete and the city
gave up its thousands who were helpless as birds
caught in a firestorm, burning from inside their skulls
and yet where gas flared, goats graze,
a mother pumps water and a boy plays.

A boy born without a nose takes a fall near a wall of painted skulls.
Under a scrap roof in a branded city his mother cleans his graze
as he sings like the birds that nest in the tower where he plays.

On Michael Longley's *Snow Water*

It drops through the letterbox in a jiffy bag.
I open it: an otter with a blue paw sidles out
shadowed by a mountain hare, ears burnt umber.

Pages reek with spraints and ebb tides.
I read it through the night, hungry for wildness,
the details of a wheatear among speedwell.

A blustery wedding day:
you pack away dead friends
among flocks of lapwings.

Achilles chases Hector to the wellheads,
pins him down like a Mayo sparrow hawk.

Let me watch the moon with you, Michael,
while we share your Silver Needles Tea,
talk geese and cranberry fields.

I will clitter the buttons of the accordion
stolen from The Yellow Bungalow,
gather up your dropped feathers.

My finches

They nip and spill all day,
gently Tarzan-swing their feeder
half hidden in the elder froth,
shower nyjer seeds on wall moss,
pepper the squishy green.

They tattle music, these gold ones
with red Kabuki demon masks
who easily upstage the grump
of three great tit fledglings
bunched on a backdrop branch.

Their effortless persistence,
their casual shift system
unflustered by rain or cats' climbs
says squander time to share
our small important lives.

For waste may be holy
when beaks are quicker than fingertips
that flit the holes of a recorder
and there have been too many months
of the chill, drenched garden.

At night, in this almost summer,
awake, forcing the old dream of flight,
I find I've grown soft feathers
resplendent with yellow wing flash
and have learnt to skim the air
        like a flat pebble.

Deep ways, sharp weather

For three weeks, the car's old currency.
It's not possible to rush at subjects; the crunch
and slide of our walk to the station takes time.
Like waiting, other life forms become important:
small dull birds loosed from the moor, pipit paupers
who beg for bread and water in quilted gardens.
Their high pipes praise a more vulnerable age
when prayer meetings migrated from farm to farm,
the doctor's mare breasted the drifts, cruel months
were lit by tallow flames and stubborn faith
coloured peat-brown rose out of the heavy book.

These off-comers alight on soft boulders of brambles
in the white-out of our neighbour's wasteland:
uprooted trees, pallets and half-burned car part boxes
tarpaulined with snowfall. Their brittle calls
prophesy to the wind, echo along the track
where, back to the last great war and fast forward,
children play over the hills, we broadcast seed by hand,
revelling in company but left to ourselves
in a silence that holds fewer and fuller words.

House and Martens

Gothic Victorian towers with a Bavarian twist,
a gate, a drive, and between manicure and moor

European swallows

white rumps, pressed squeaks
splashed with blue-black

pied doctors from Venetian carnival

good and bad angels rolled into one
tumbling the sky

winging it with farm dances of the Fifties:
The Chitter, The Squint, The Splat

fly eaters with mid drop catches
outbirding Superman.

*

At the lawn's edge, he's forking hay in shorts
and his implement is all wood, even the tines.
He's stocky, shirtless and from near her country.

She makes a slow walk, truanting from the kitchen,
steps out like a heavy horse from beneath the portico
and squelches across the grass, sodden as summer.

He takes the sandwich, thick with leaves and spreads.
She watches him chomp, tugs at her ill-fitting blouse
and savours the undertones: wet heat, sex in the haze.

He preens moves from his courtship ritual:
The Ogle, The Vilnius Gawp, The Try-It-On.
She replies with The Estonian Tilt; a lowering of eyes.

And all the long short time the oddly spelt birds
flutter above them, tails short and forked,
accelerated beats to the minute, like their hearts,

The scene ends without the wing-melt of a touch.
He bends over a machine, tinkers with the under-parts.
The flock 'V's it back to under eaves, to spit and stalks.

Fascinator

Reptilian – chameleon's crest.
Or avian – jungle fowl
hunted and plucked,
arranged, accessorised
for a stomp in the clearing.

In your hair, a hushed bounce
of wire and aqua-marine,
an air net of bird shake,
a peck and pock of flutter,
leaf curls in a puff of breeze.

A signifier, at this love fest
where everyone's tooled up
in tightness and hire
for a nest leaving;
a quiver of kept-in feelings.

We preserve it, like a bouquet
or champagne flute, in the car boot
as we criss-cross the country
from strawberry farm to cast-iron pier;
fish scale sky, deep blue sea-peas.

Proud feathers will drift in dust,
occasionally flutter on the shelf
before they become *planta nocturna,*
wardrobe foliage, a still jig,
exquisite flight piece, memory wisp.